To: The People's Trust for Endangered Species
Hares are becoming increasingly scarce in Britain.
If you would like to help, write to:

PTES
15 Cloisters House
8 Battersea Park Road
London SW8 4BG

CW

Designed by Mark Mills

Printed and bound by Proost, Belgium
for the publishers Piccadilly Press Ltd,
5 Castle Road, London NW1 8PR

1 3 5 7 9 10 8 6 4 2

A catalogue record for this book is available from the British Library

ISBNs: 1 85340 604 X paperback
1 85340 609 0 hardback

Wishes For You

Adèle Geras

illustrated by
Cliff Wright

PICCADILLY PRESS ~ LONDON

I wish you . . .

Light from behind the hill
spilling into the sky.

Kisses to wake you,

warm sun on your face.

A path that goes from here
to everywhere.

Daydreams like birds
unfolding wide white wings.

A kind gaze following you
as you walk.

A smile to smile at when you
turn your head.

Trees wide enough
for you to
hide behind
and drifting
shadows, pieces
of the dark . . .

. . . which vanish
as the sun
moves through
the leaves.

Small pools to splash in when the
rain comes down.
A dancing stream to follow with
your dance.

Your own hands strong to pile up stones you find into a tower high enough to climb . . .

. . . and arms outstretched
to catch you if you fall.

Someone to tell you words
for everything.
Laughter to join your laughter,
songs to sing.

A quilt to cover you
and all your dreams,

warm in your bed,

safe through the quiet night.

Darkness and moonlight,

your star in the sky.